BUILDING the PAST

by Miranda Spekes • illustrated by Linda Ayriss

CHAPTERS

Introduction 2
The Parthenon 3
Greek Columns 5
Roman Innovations 7
The Colosseum 10
The Pantheon 11
Why Imitate the Past? 14

Orlando Boston Dallas Chicago San Diego

Visit *The Learning Site!*
www.harcourtschool.com

Introduction

Our world—with its busy freeways and tall skyscrapers—seems far removed from ancient Athens and Rome. It is one thing to read that the modern world shows the influence of Greek and Roman culture; it is another thing entirely to *find* the results of that influence.

Just about every city in the United States has traces of Greek and Roman influence, particularly in the architecture of government buildings. Certain details remind us of Greek and Roman architecture, such as arches, domes, rows of stone columns with a squat triangle called a *pediment* on top, and wide stone porches and steps leading

The Parthenon today

up to the main doors. All of these details serve as emblems of ancient Greece and Rome. Let's look at three of the most famous buildings of the ancient world: the Parthenon, the Colosseum, and the Pantheon.

THE PARTHENON

The Parthenon, the most famous ancient Greek building still standing today, loomed over Athens in ancient times. This large temple on a hill called the *Acropolis* took fifteen years to build. Visible from just about any place in the city, the Parthenon was the home of a forty-foot statue of the goddess Athena, for whom Athens is named.

The Largest Temple

The largest temple built by the ancient Greeks was the Artemision, or the Temple of Artemis, one of the Seven Wonders of the Ancient World. The Artemision took 220 years to build and was 425 feet long, 220 feet wide, and more than 60 feet tall. An impressive 127 columns held up a roof made of cedar, which sheltered a statue of the Greek goddess Artemis. Unfortunately, the temple was destroyed in 262 B.C., so artists and archaeologists have had to reconstruct in drawings what the Temple of Artemis might have looked like.

Athenians were great lovers of art. They felt that everything around them, even the buildings they lived in, should be pleasing to the eye. Therefore, when the builders set about constructing the Parthenon, they took special care that the building would look beautiful.

To the naked eye, the Parthenon *appears* perfect. The sides seem to form razor-sharp lines, and the columns run straight up and down—yet the eye lies. There is no truly straight line in the entire building. The corners of the Parthenon sag down, and the columns lean in. The builders made it this way on purpose. They knew that the human eye distorts what it sees. To make the huge temple pleasing to the eye, they had to make secret adjustments.

The builders wanted the sides of the temple to look straight. To the eye, however, perfectly straight lines appear to sag in the middle. Therefore, the builders made the sides rise up slightly in the center. The sides of the building are actually about four-and-a-half inches higher in the center than in the corners!

The builders also made the columns bulge out in the middle and taper a bit at the tops and the bottoms, because to someone looking up at it, a straight column gives the illusion of being thinner in the middle. The builders also made the columns lean in a little bit; otherwise, the human eye would see the building as top-heavy.

All of these small adjustments gave the Parthenon a look of elegance and balance. Twenty-five hundred years later, we still view the Parthenon as one of the most graceful structures ever built.

Greek Columns

Part of the outward beauty of the Parthenon is due to its aesthetic simplicity. Despite the temple's large size, the builders followed the rules and layout of much smaller temples. Both the Parthenon and smaller temples were built as rectangles, with long sides and a short front and back. All had porches in front, which met a flight of wide steps; a ring of columns all around the building; and a central room that held the statue of a god or goddess.

Doric column

The two most popular kinds of columns used by Greek builders were called Doric and Ionic. The Doric column was sturdy and thick, while the Ionic column was thinner. The tops of the columns, called *capitals*, were also different. Doric columns were topped by a simple capital that looked like a stone cushion. Ionic columns had a more complex capital decorated with curling scrolls. Both kinds of columns had deep vertical grooves called *flutes* carved into them. These grooves caught light and shadow and made the columns look more interesting.

To make the columns, the builders used a kind of stone called marble. They carved the columns in sections that were easy to move. Once they had the sections where they wanted them, the builders stacked ten or twelve of them on top of one another, connecting them with metal rods down the center. The outer columns of the Parthenon had to be 34 feet tall. These columns were so well built that they still stand today.

Ionic column

Greek post-and-beam architecture

ROMAN INNOVATIONS

When the Romans made Greece a province of their empire in about 146 B.C., one of the things they brought back to Rome was the Greek style of architecture. The Romans loved to build things. They built roads, stadiums, bridges, and buildings that, after 2,000 years, are still standing all over Europe.

Roman architects also had their own great ideas. For example, because of their concern for hygiene, the Romans developed aqueducts to carry clean water throughout Rome. One of the greatest architectural innovations of the Romans, however, was the arch. The Romans were not the first people to use arches in their buildings, but they were the first to use them often and well.

Greek temples, such as the Parthenon, were built in what is called post-and-beam style. That is, a flat beam was put on top of each pair of columns, and the roof rested on the beams. The beams were heavy, however, and the roof was often heavier still. Therefore, many columns were needed to carry the weight of the beams and the roof. The bigger the temple, the more columns were needed inside and outside, and the more cluttered the temple looked.

As an alternative to the post-and-beam style, the Romans perfected the use of the arch. An arch is a half-circle made out of wedge-shaped blocks. Arches are stronger than post-and-beam construction, because the weight of the blocks pushing down on the wedges forces the wedges more tightly together, thus making the arch

Weight forces wedges tight against one another.

Weight pushes this way.

The weight is shifted to the side supports.

Roman arch

stronger. A building that uses arches can weigh much more than a building made with post-and-beam construction because the more weight put on an arch, the stronger the arch becomes.

Arches are practical for another reason, too. The many columns needed to support a post-and-beam style roof don't leave a lot of open space within a building. A roof that uses arches can span a greater space. The supports for the arch stand at the outside edge of the room, so the center can be empty and open.

In addition to arches, the Romans also used something called a *vault*. They found that they could make an arched tunnel (or *barrel vault*) that would support a lot of weight.

These two ideas—the arch and the vault—made it possible for the Romans to build huge structures, such as the Colosseum.

The Colosseum today. There are eighty arches ringing the bottom. Tunnels between the walls are barrel vaults.

The Colosseum

People watched the Roman Games in this enormous stadium in the center of Rome. Similar to the earlier open-air theaters in Greece but built on a much larger scale, the Colosseum could hold as many as 50,000 people. Unlike the open-air theaters, the Colosseum was free standing. That is, it was not built into a hillside that provided outside support for the many levels of seating. Instead, a system of arches and vaults supported the Colosseum's 400,000 tons of stone as well as the weight of the people who sat in its seats.

You can see how important the arch is to the design of the Colosseum by looking at a picture of it. The arches visible on each story opened onto corridors—actually barrel vaults—that ringed the entire building. These corridors are visible in the space between the outer wall and the inner wall of the stadium. In addition, large vaults crisscrossed beneath the floor where the games were held.

What about the Greek-style columns visible on the outside walls of the Colosseum? How much weight do those support? The answer is none. The columns are there simply for decoration, much like the mosaics inside the building or the statues that, in ancient times, stood in the arches on the upper levels.

The Romans borrowed from the architecture of their conquered neighbors, the Greeks, and incorporated various elements into their own buildings. The Roman love of Greek architecture is visible in another famous Roman building, the Pantheon.

THE PANTHEON

From the front, the Pantheon looks somewhat like a Greek temple. Steps lead up to a wide stone porch. Eight columns on the porch support a pediment. Beyond the columns is the door to the temple. Once inside, however, it becomes clear just how different the Pantheon is from Greek temples.

For one thing, this Roman temple is home to the statues of seven gods, not *one* as in Greek culture. In fact, the name Pantheon means "of all the gods."

The inside of the temple is a wonder. The center contains a huge, round room called a *rotunda*, topped by a big dome. At the very top of the dome is a round hole that lets in sunlight. The floor of the rotunda measures more than 140 feet across and is set with pretty mosaic tiles. Statues of the gods stand against the walls. The floor between the statues contains nothing but wide, open space, because no columns are needed to hold up the roof. From any point in the room, you can see every other point. Over the course of each day, as the sun moves across the sky, a shaft of light moves through the room, so the rotunda has light all day long.

Roomy and elegant, the Pantheon is ancient Rome's most famous structure. It is also one of the most imitated in the world.

Inside the Pantheon

Rome's Pantheon as it looks today. The front of the building recalls Greek construction, but the dome, or *rotunda*, is a Roman innovation.

Another Roman invention, cement, made domes such as the Pantheon's possible. A mix of limestone, sand, and water, cement was first used in about 400 B.C. Cement made building architectural elements such as arches easier. Builders poured cement into molds, and, when it dried, it was as strong as stone. With the right mold, cement could also be made into just about any shape. To make the dome on top of the Pantheon, the builders made a wooden frame and coated it with cement. When the cement dried, the builders removed the frame. In the same way that stone arches are made stronger by their own weight, cement also becomes stronger when used in arches and domes.

The Pantheon was unlike any building before it, but since its time many buildings have copied its features, such as its dome.

Supreme Court

The Capitol

Why Imitate the Past?

Why did the Roman builders want to imitate Greek temples? Why did the people who constructed the buildings in our nation's capital include so many references to Greek and Roman buildings? Is something more than architectural beauty behind these reminders of Greece and Rome in our public buildings?

These two cultures also gave the world ideas about government. Ancient Greece is considered the birthplace of democracy. All citizens (free men) could vote, and any of them were elegible to serve in the assembly. The idea of a republican form of government came from the Romans. Before Rome ruled an empire, it had been a republic. Roman citizens voted for people who would then

Lincoln Memorial

Jefferson Memorial

represent them in the government. Both of these ideas greatly influenced the design of the U.S. government.

So many buildings in Washington, D.C., contain elements of Greek and Roman architecture, it is difficult to list them all. A short list might include the Supreme Court, the Capitol building, the Department of Commerce, the Lincoln Memorial, and the Jefferson Memorial.

When architects were designing the buildings for Washington, D.C., they chose the Parthenon and the Pantheon as models for a couple of reasons. First, using classical architectural styles made a young country like the United States seem more worldly.

The other reason is more complex. The Parthenon and Pantheon were temples, but people did not gather in these places to pray or to worship. Instead, each building was a symbolic home of gods or goddesses.

In the United States our government buildings are the "temples" of important ideas. The architects wanted visitors to feel what the ancient Greeks and Romans felt, that they were in the presence of something great. Borrowing from the architecture of the Greeks and Romans helps remind us that great ideas live on in history. The United States has blended not only the architecture of two great cultures into its own buildings but also the beliefs and practices of two of the most important concepts of government in history: democracy and a republican form of government.

The White House